RYUHO OKAWA

On

CARBON FOOTPRINTS REDUCING

WHY GRETA GETS ANGRY?

HS PRESS

Contents

Preface 7

On Carbon footprints reducing
—Why Greta gets angry?

1 Who Gave Spiritual Influence On Miss Greta
   Thunberg? 12

2 The Spirit's Warning: Noah's Great Flood Will
   Occur Again

   The purpose is "climate justice" 18

   America is "the champion of the devils" 26

   I am Noah 31

3 "Human Beings Are the Enemy of the Earth;
   I Want to Stop the Civilization"

   Happiness means to harmonize with nature 37

   Science has one conclusion; there is no freedom of
   academy 45

   Saying "no" to nuclear power generation and the
   Industrial Revolution 49

3

4 Which God Does the Spirit Believe In?

I can't see the figure of God, only the voice comes
down 55

"Space people? I don't know" 59

My God is older than Israel's god, it's an ancient god of
Scandinavia 61

5 Asking about Japan and China

Xi Jinping is "a devil" 66

He is not sure if he is the real Noah or not 69

"Japanese are bad people" 72

His recognition of Odin 78

Technology will destroy the Earth 81

6 Another Spirit behind Miss Greta Thunberg's
Actions

The spirit who calls himself the "only God" appears 84

The leader of the Russian Revolution declares the
resurrection of Russia 88

7 Why the Spirit Wants to Spread the Global
   Warming Theory

Why he wants to stop the CO_2 emission of advanced
countries 93

Greta will be "a new Christ" 99

"Climate change revolution" for the people of the north
part of the Earth 102

8 After the Spiritual Interviews 107

Afterword 111

About the Author 113

What is El Cantare? 114

What is a Spiritual Message? 116

About Happy Science 120

Contact Information 124

About HS Press 126

Books by Ryuho Okawa 127

Music by Ryuho Okawa 132

* The lecture was conducted in English.

Preface

Just recently, the 16-year-old Swedish girl Greta Thunberg gave a mad speech at the UN meeting for environmental problems. She is famous for starting demonstrations of millions all over the world.

She may think that her worst enemy is President Trump, and also be angry about Japan's no-reaction attitude. It took her 15 days to cross the Atlantic Ocean by yacht, and she joined in the UN meeting, stared at President Trump, scolded the adults, and said angrily about giving back the children their future. I must not be the only one who felt she had "something" that peaceful environmentalists don't have. In this book, we did a spiritual reading on the being who is guiding her.

In conclusion, I want to say there is a cycle to global warming, and occurrence of CO_2 is not the only reason. Ancient Earth was a burning Hell covered in magma. Due to volcanic eruption, the volcanic ash and CO_2 covered the earth. Now, the global warming's last stage of the 10,000 year cycle is coming. Climate change causes the transition in civilization. However, it is also one of the providences of God. Ms. Greta and her supporters should know this.

Ryuho Okawa
Master & CEO of Happy Science Group
Oct. 25, 2019

On Carbon footprints reducing

–Why Greta gets angry?

Recorded September 25, 2019
Special Lecture Hall, Happy Science,
Japan

Greta Thunberg (2003 - Present)

An environmental activist from Stockholm, Sweden. She began the school climate strike in August 2018. It became a worldwide movement, and on September 20, 2019, protests were held in many places across the world, with more than four million young people participating in 163 countries. She gave a speech at the UN Climate Action Summit three days later on September 23. Her SNS accounts state that she has Asperger's Syndrome.

Interviewers from Happy Science[*]

Masayuki Isono

Executive Director
Chief of Overseas Missionary Work Promotion Office
Deputy Chief Secretary, First Secretarial Division
Religious Affairs Headquarters

Motohisa Fujii

Associate Director
Special Assistant to Religious Affairs Headquarters
Director General of International Politics Division

Toshimitsu Yoshii

General Manager of International Politics Division
Religious Affairs Headquarters

*No statements made by the spirits in this book
reflect statements actually made by Miss Greta Thunberg herself.*

*The opinions of the spirit do not necessarily reflect those of Happy Science Group.
For the mechanism behind spiritual messages, see end section.*

---

[*] Interviewers are listed in the order that they appear in the transcript.
Their professional titles represent their positions at the time of the interview.

1

Who Gave Spiritual Influence On Miss Greta Thunberg?

RYUHO OKAWA

Thank you so much for coming today. Good evening.

One problem has attracted me. At the conference of the UN, only 16-year-old, young girl named Greta Thunberg [see Figure 1] from Sweden made

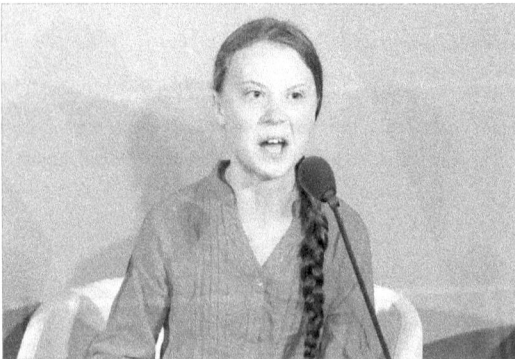

Figure 1.
Greta Thunberg giving a speech at the United Nations Climate Action Summit on September 23, 2019 in New York, U.S.A.

a small speech, and it was broadcasted through a lot of newspapers and on TV. It was a very, very small speech, but I felt something difficult and mad thing about that. What she said is a good opinion or not, or in another way, I will say, does it come from God or a god-like existence, or only from herself or her guardian spirit? Or, is there any other influence on her? She is a small girl, but she stared at Mr. President Donald Trump and it's very, how do I say, angry god or devil-like face, so we need a conclusion, and this is our mission. I think so.

The world is getting a great impact from her speech because this is regarding the global warming, a very famous problem, and it's very difficult to realize in reality. Every country has its own reason to reduce or to produce CO_2, so it's not so easy to make a promise with her.

This only 16-year-old young girl came from Stockholm, Sweden. And from the U.K., United Kingdom, to New York, she used a yacht, by dint of electric power of wind and solar panel, and it took 15 days. I think it's brave, but if we, all the grown-up people, used such kind of wind and solar panel only, we cannot keep our modern civilization.

She got very angry about that, and she also said that, "My message is that we'll be watching you!" It means "watching grown-up people who easily speak false things," she wants to say so. "This is all wrong. I shouldn't be up here. I should be back in school on the other side of the ocean, yet you all come to us young people for hope. How dare you!" And she said, "You have stolen my dreams and my childhood with your empty words," like that.

Some people say she has Asperger Syndrome and ADHD or another syndrome, but she started this global warming problem in 2018, and next 2019, she made a speech at Davos (World Economic Forum Annual Meeting). She already is a Nobel Peace Prize laureate nominee, and *TIME* magazine has chosen her as one of the "100 Most Influential People of the World." And she did the speech this September 23.

So, on Greta's carbon footprints* reducing, or in another old-fashioned saying, carbon dioxide or CO_2 emission problem, is it true or not, I have something to say, but firstly, I'll make a spiritual reading of her. "What influenced her? Is this her guardian spirit or guardian angel, or near-God angel, or quite opposite to them, or alien-like existence has some power on her?" I want to know about that.

This is very important for our 21st century's people, so I have an opinion, but before that, I want to check, "Is this just her soul brother's† opinion, or another big guy or spiritual beings, are there several, or alien-like spiritual being?" I want

---

* The amount of carbon dioxide (CO_2) emitted by products or services. It includes getting raw materials, manufacturing, distribution, sales, and disposal. "Carbon" means CO_2, and "footprint" means the amount of CO_2 emission.

† In the fundamental meaning, the human soul has six parts; one core soul and five branch souls, and they are called "soul siblings." They are a part of the soul of a living person, and are also called the subconscious. See Ryuho Okawa, *The Laws of the Sun* (New York: IRH Press, 2018).

to know about that. So, I'll call the one who gave her most powerful influence, so please check it. As a 16-year-old student girl, I think it's difficult to speak more than five or ten minutes, but if another greater one is with her, it will have some great opinion, I mean, what is the real aim of this opinion? I want to know about this.

OK then, I'll call. [*To the interviewers*] Do you understand what I mean? OK? Almost 77 countries have promised that they will stop emission of CO_2 by 2050, but she said, "I cannot believe that." OK. I'll then examine.

What was the spiritual influence on
Miss Greta Thunberg at the UN conference?
Could I ask who has most powerful influence on
Miss Greta Thunberg?
Could you come down here to Happy Science
And appear before us?
Are you her soul brother or guardian spirit,
Or another one?
I don't know, I just ask

What is most important influence
And who made influence on her.

[*17 seconds of silence.*]

2

The Spirit's Warning:
Noah's Great Flood Will Occur Again

The purpose is "climate justice"

SPIRIT 1
[*Coughs.*]

ISONO
Hello.

SPIRIT 1
[*Coughs.*]

ISONO
Hello.

SPIRIT 1
Hmm? [*Coughs.*]

ISONO

Can you hear me? Can you speak?

SPIRIT 1

Hmm?

ISONO

Can you speak?

SPIRIT 1

I cannot believe you.

ISONO

Why?

SPIRIT 1

Who are you?

ISONO

No, no. Who are *you*?

SPIRIT 1

Who are you? Who are you?

ISONO

We are Happy Science staff members...

SPIRIT 1

I don't know. I don't know Happy Science. Who are you?

ISONO

We are Japanese.

SPIRIT 1

Japanese?

ISONO

Yes.

SPIRIT 1

Japan is a bad country.

ISONO

No. Japan is a good country.

SPIRIT 1

No. You have a lot of CO_2 emission.

ISONO

Yes, but...

SPIRIT 1

Do you know Mr. Prime Minister Abe's gigantic balloon in front of the city hall or library?* Some people hate Prime Minister Abe. You, Japanese, did bad things to climate change. Hmm!

FUJII

Are you the person who made a speech at the United Nations conference?

SPIRIT 1

Of course! Of course!

---

* On September 23, 2019 in New York, U.S.A., climate activists launched a balloon of Japanese Prime Minister Shinzo Abe, protesting to the Japanese government for being the only G7 country to support coal power generation.

ISONO

So, are you Miss Greta Thunberg?

SPIRIT 1

Hm?

ISONO

Are you Miss Greta Thunberg herself?

SPIRIT 1

Hmm... I'm with her. I'm with her. Almost, yeah, almost, I am almost Greta.

ISONO

I think you are a guardian spirit of Miss Greta Thunberg.

SPIRIT 1

"Guardian spirit", hmm...

ISONO

Guardian spirit is a part of her subconsciousness.

SPIRIT 1

Hmm...

ISONO

So, you are a part of her.

SPIRIT 1

Not the subconsciousness. I am the... the teacher of her superficial consciousness.

ISONO

Uh huh. So, you gave her inspiration or some instruction, what to say at the United Nations. Correct?

SPIRIT 1

Correct.

ISONO

OK.

SPIRIT 1

Uh huh.

ISONO

Miss Greta's speech at the United Nations made a huge impact across the globe.

SPIRIT 1

Uh huh.

ISONO

And I was so shocked to watch your speech. You used very harsh and aggressive words, and you criticized global leaders, that they are liars.

SPIRIT 1

Hmm, yeah, liars. True. Truly, truly.

ISONO

What was the purpose or aim of your speech at the United Nations?

SPIRIT 1

Climate justice.

ISONO

Climate justice?

SPIRIT 1

Hmm.

ISONO

What do you think is climate justice?

SPIRIT 1

People will die completely in the near future, in this century, so we must stop it.

ISONO

We must stop emission of CO_2?

SPIRIT 1

Yeah, yeah.

America is "the champion of the devils"

ISONO

Then, are you saying we shouldn't or we must not use any electricity made by fossil fuel? Or, are you proposing that all people around the world should use solar power or wind power? Are you insisting so?

SPIRIT 1

The resource is not the problem. We will be under the sea in the near future, when I will be grown up, maybe 40 or 50, or like that. We, Swedish, will be also under the sea. So, a lot of countries of the south part of this hemisphere, Northern Hemisphere, will go down into the sea. And there occurred a lot of hurricanes, typhoons, or tsunami-like weather problems.

So, it's time to stop. You have much concern about earning money, or only the fairy tale of global development, or your-country-only-development like the devil Donald Trump says,

"Only America First." America is the champion of the devils. He insists so. We must fight against that kind of evil people.

ISONO

Why do you hate wealth so much?

SPIRIT 1

No, no, I don't hate wealth. "Our lives, the lives of the earthlings, are heavier than money." I'm just saying so.

FUJII

I think you are more than a 16-year-old girl. Why do you have so much knowledge on global warming and so on?

SPIRIT 1

I studied.

FUJII

Where did you learn that?

SPIRIT 1

"Where"?

FUJII

Yes.

SPIRIT 1

At school, and in my room of my house. Yeah. I have keen attention about that. We are on the upper side of Europe, and around the North Pole area, already, the huge icebergs are becoming just water, and white bears are swimming in the water. Not on the icebergs, but just swimming like a dog. It's very much a problem.

So, it will occur, I mean the great flood. When Noah... you know Noah, written in the Old Testament? It is Noah's time again, and there will occur Noah's-like global flood. At that time, the height of the water of the sea came to more than the middle of the Ararat mountains. So, at that time, the height of the sky — no, the height of the sea became more than 2,000 meters. So, I'm very afraid about that. I am the Noah of the modern times, I think so.

YOSHII

In the age of Noah, was there any civilization to use CO_2?

SPIRIT 1

Yeah. Noah's... yeah, yeah, there already occurred CO_2 problem. People used a lot of fire. Now, you can see only desert in the Middle East, for example, around Lebanon, there used to be a great, huge forest. But now, it reduced to a small place, and there are a mountain of sands around there and around the African continent.

YOSHII

I think you insist the justification of science. In some speeches, you mentioned that you'd like to "unite behind the science." I'm wondering, there are various theories in science, so there is some doubt, right?

SPIRIT 1

Doubt? Yeah, doubt.

YOSHII

Yeah, there is some doubt about climate change.

SPIRIT 1

Bad people doubt, yeah doubt.

YOSHII

Oh, yeah. Currently, the climate change "is not necessarily caused by CO_2, other factors make climate change happen," so there are various theories.* Why do you push on one extreme theory, about only reducing CO_2 emission?

---

* It is said that there are different causes to global warming, for example, more methane, more or fewer sunspots, change in the ozone layer, and change in amount of cosmic rays hitting Earth.

SPIRIT 1

Hmm, because of my old memory, maybe. At that time, I warned about the rain. "There will come a lot of rain from heaven, from the sky, and there will be the ocean," I prophesied like that, but no one heard about that. Only I, my family, and my animals could save our lives. This is written in the Old Testament. So, I warn again. Yeah, it's time. It's time to perish you, earthlings, again.

I am Noah

YOSHII

At that time, you were a supporter of Noah?

SPIRIT 1

I am (Noah)! I was!

YOSHII

OK, uh huh.

ISONO

Are you Noah, himself?

SPIRIT 1

Yes, I was.

ISONO

You are? You are Noah?

SPIRIT 1

Noah. And I just heard the voice of God, "Noah, save people, save animals!" But no one heard me, and I made my ship and I lived longer than the other tribes' people. They didn't believe in God.

FUJII

Where are you living now in the Spirit World?

SPIRIT 1

Huh? Spirit World?

FUJII

What kind of Spirit World are you living in now?

SPIRIT 1

What kind of Spirit World?

FUJII

You mean you are living in this world?

SPIRIT 1

What kind of Spirit World... what do you mean?
What kind of Spirit World... what do you mean?

ISONO

Do you live by yourself or with somebody?

FUJII

I think you are not Greta Thunberg, herself.

SPIRIT 1

Umm, I'm, I'm male. Yeah, yeah, yeah. I'm not female, I'm male, but...

FUJII

Not a girl?

SPIRIT 1

I am also Greta. I don't know exactly, but we are very much combined.

ISONO

If you are the real Noah, then why did you choose Greta as a speaker for your voice? She's just a 16-year-old girl. She had no influence before she began her activity. Then, why she...

SPIRIT 1

She's such kind of... So, that's the reason she's the prophet.

ISONO

Are you sure?

SPIRIT 1

I'm sure.

ISONO

Are you the real Noah?

SPIRIT 1

I hope so.

ISONO

You hope so?

FUJII

You said you have a long-term memory. How long?

SPIRIT 1

Huh?

FUJII

How long of a memory do you have? A thousand years or more?

SPIRIT 1

It's about 4,000 years ago. Yeah.

FUJII

Four thousand years ago, you were a man?

SPIRIT 1

A man.

FUJII

You were a man.

SPIRIT 1

And my descendants, my children are the origin of the modern people.

3

"Human Beings Are
The Enemy of the Earth;
I Want to Stop the Civilization"

Happiness means to harmonize with nature

YOSHII

You mentioned that in the age of Noah, the cause
of big flooding was brought by using fire, you said.
Using fire.

SPIRIT 1

Yeah, yeah. Like the Amazon area now, you know?
Brazilian problem (of rain forest fires).

YOSHII

And now, you are strongly insisting that reducing
CO_2 emissions is necessary, so is using electricity
related to faith in God?

SPIRIT 1

No, no. Using electricity is not required in a civilization. It leads to another big war. If you don't use such kind of huge electricity, you will never fight against each other in every country, but your fuel supplying can make it easy to cause greater wars. So, the problem is China, Russia, the United States of America, the EU, Saudi Arabia, Iran, or almost all of them. Don't use electricity from oil, or gas, or another fossil.

YOSHII

So, you mean to stop using technology?

SPIRIT 1

Yeah.

YOSHII

Then, what kind of happiness are you aiming to spread?

SPIRIT 1

Live happily with nature.

YOSHII

With nature, I see.

ISONO

But the number of population in the world is increasing rapidly in this century. And people...

SPIRIT 1

That's a problem. More than 7 billion, 7.6 or 7.7 bill...

ISONO

So, do you believe that increasing the population is an evil thing?

SPIRIT 1

Evil! Yeah, evil.

ISONO

So, you hope that population should decrease or the civilization should collapse or decline?

SPIRIT 1

I think that the humankind is the most dreadful enemy to the Earth, and the lives of plants and animals, and the air or atmosphere of this Earth. So, human beings became the enemy of the Earth.

YOSHII

In this case, what is the reason for humans to be born on the earth?

SPIRIT 1

Hmm... hmm... I think we, younger people, should have hope for the future, but older people are using a lot of fuels and making CO_2 emissions and they are killing our future. That's a problem. We need our future, but we don't need old people, so the people who are more than 30 years old, these people are evil now.

YOSHII

I think in pursuing your future, the current younger people are living just in harmony with nature.

SPIRIT 1

Uh, harmonize with nature.

YOSHII

So, I think there are few options to live. Is it OK? Too narrow...

SPIRIT 1

Live like Swedish people. We don't need the United States of America. We don't need Japan. We don't need China. We don't need Russia. We don't need Singapore or Hong Kong or other advanced countries.

FUJII

In short, you don't like civilization.

SPIRIT 1

Yeah. Truly.

FUJII

You want to stop civilization.

SPIRIT 1

Yeah, truly, truly.

FUJII

That's the reason why you...

SPIRIT 1

It's just making the huge Tower of Babylon (Tower of Babel),* you know? People built a huge tower, and God got angry and destroyed the tower. People can no longer speak one language, so they act differently, and there occurred the discriminations

---

* A tower mentioned in the Book of Genesis in the Old Testament. After Noah's Great Flood, humans tried to build a tower that would reach the heavens in order to prevent themselves from separating into different races. But Yahweh saw that and got angry; he brought confusion to the human language and prevented people from communicating with each other. So, they stopped building the tower and scattered across the world.

between people. So, we must eliminate or we must choose some countries which can survive.

ISONO

This might be a difficult question for you, but what do you think is the purpose of life in this world?

SPIRIT 1

Purpose of life?

ISONO

Why are we, human beings, born onto this earth?

SPIRIT 1

Hmm. Live happily with animals and plants and nature. Yeah, this is the hope of God.

YOSHII

What kind of role have you played as a spiritual being? You are a guardian of the earth or plant or forest? I mean, you are not a guardian of human beings.

SPIRIT 1

In Sweden, there are a lot of fairies or natural spirits, but they are at the cliff of perishing. People of modern society are killing these kinds of natural spirits or fairies. So, I have much concern about that. Your God, the God who is leading modern society, modern civilization, in another name, might be Baal*; the name which is Baal, earning money only. It's bad faith, I think.

ISONO

So, who is your God? Who do you believe in? What do you believe in?

SPIRIT 1

Uh... I cannot explain correctly, but I said Baal, you know? Baal is the criminal of destroying the Lebanon forest, and he made Mediterranean areas

---

* A false god in the ancient Middle East. It is an evil god of commerce, a god of economic supremacy, and also called the god of Mammon. It is also called Beelzebub or Belial.

trade and earned a lot of money. So, you are the supporters of that kind of evil god.

Science has one conclusion; There is no freedom of academy

YOSHII

I think, in technology, through making a progress, humans can feel happiness. So, I think there is a way to make nature and technology compatible.

SPIRIT 1

No, no, no, no, no.

YOSHII

No?

SPIRIT 1

Science, science. Believe in science. Learn science. These 30 years' scientific development.

YOSHII

Yeah, I respect your opinion.

SPIRIT 1

The conclusion is one.

YOSHII

But I think even in science, there is the freedom of academy, so there are various theories.

SPIRIT 1

No, no, no. Freedom of academy, no, no, no. One conclusion.

FUJII

Like President Trump, many people don't believe the global warming theory.

SPIRIT 1

Yeah, Donald Trump is the top devil, top level of devils.

FUJII

Global warming is just a hypothesis.

SPIRIT 1

Hypothesis?

FUJII

Yes.

SPIRIT 1

No, no, no. It's a conclusion of modern science.

YOSHII

What makes you strongly believe in that conclusion?

SPIRIT 1

Hmm... because I got the mission from God.

FUJII

Mission for what?

SPIRIT 1

God.

FUJII

To destroy the world and civilization?

SPIRIT 1

Yeah. God says, they, "they" means you, civilized countries, are hypocrites! It's you. If you don't obey God's order, you will be destroyed, and the global flooding will kill you all!

YOSHII

In your conclusion, I think human beings are in the direction of disappearing from the Earth. Is it your conclusion?

SPIRIT 1

Yeah, if you don't follow God, or God's order, you will be ruined. Yeah.

Saying "no" to nuclear power generation
And the Industrial Revolution

ISONO

By the way, what do you think about nuclear power generation?

SPIRIT 1

Nuclear power? No.

ISONO

It doesn't emit any carbon dioxide.

SPIRIT 1

I don't like. I don't like it because, nuclear power will make electricity of course, but it will be a new weapon for killing a lot of people, and will make a lot of fire in the world. So, it also must be destroyed, or must disappear from this world. You live with vegetables and small animals. That is heaven.

FUJII

So, you mean, we human beings should live like animals? Is that your conclusion?

SPIRIT 1

No, no, no. Not. Gentle animals.

FUJII

Gentle animals.

SPIRIT 1

Uh huh. Not the attacking animals which kill other animals.

FUJII

Without electricity?

SPIRIT 1

Without electricity? Hmm...

FUJII

You mean that?

SPIRIT 1

Yeah. Just eat vegetables or fruits, or like that.

ISONO

If you could realize your plan, there would be a massacre, a great massacre.

SPIRIT 1

Great massacre? Massacre?

ISONO

I mean, a great number of people would die because of your plan.

SPIRIT 1

Because they are criminals.

ISONO

So, do you agree that criminals should die?

SPIRIT 1

Yeah, yeah. It's God's will. In the age of Noah, almost everybody died.

ISONO

Do you think it is really God's hope or God's desire?

SPIRIT 1

Yeah.

ISONO

To kill people?

SPIRIT 1

God seeks for one truth, so it must be the conclusion. One conclusion. Please follow me. I am the prophet, and my disciples, only, can survive this age and live the 22nd century. You all are "good-bye" people.

YOSHII

I'm wondering if you have more than 4,000 years of history.

SPIRIT 1

Yeah.

YOSHII

Yeah? So, what kind of movements have you taught or have you led? Now, you are teaching Greta Thunberg.

SPIRIT 1

Uh huh.

YOSHII

But I think after the Industrial Revolution from the U.K., various technologies have been occurring. But you hate that. So, I think you taught the movement...

SPIRIT 1

I want to deny the Industrial Revolution. That's bad. That's evil. That's a deed of Satan.

FUJII

When was the best age for humanity? Stone age or so?

SPIRIT 1

Hmm... The countries just limited to Sweden-like landscape and population and food, that's heaven. Yeah, God's heaven.

4

Which God Does
The Spirit Believe In?

I can't see the figure of God,
Only the voice comes down

ISONO

Do you have any friends or any supporters?

SPIRIT 1

Yeah, a lot of supporters. More than four million supporters.

YOSHII

So, you are a kind of guru of environmentalists.

SPIRIT 1

Yes. Yeah, yeah. Eco-religion guru, yeah.

YOSHII

So, your purpose is to disturb the progress of technology.

SPIRIT 1

Disturb the progress of... Do you like machines or a lot of fuel or that kind of technology which can kill a lot of people, and like people to change their behavior into a lion's, or lion-like activity, and don't seek for peace? Is that right?

YOSHII

So, your God is related to the being who destroys the Tower of Babel or other civilizations' legacies?

SPIRIT 1

Yeah. God says that 100 million population is the limit.

FUJII

Are you receiving message directly from God?

SPIRIT 1

Yeah, God. From God. My God.

FUJII

What's the name of God?

SPIRIT 1

My God?

FUJII

Yes.

SPIRIT 1

The name of my God? I don't know the real name of God, might be... He might be Yahweh. I think so. Yahweh.

FUJII

What does he look like?

SPIRIT 1

What he looks like? Old man. Yeah. Old, old man with a stick.

FUJII

Bright or not bright?

SPIRIT 1

What do you mean?

FUJII

Like lightening. How do you feel about him?

SPIRIT 1

He is quite above the sky, so I can't see well. Only the voice, the voice of God comes down to me.

ISONO

So, you can't see God? You can't see the image of God, you can only hear the voice of God?

SPIRIT 1

Yeah, spiritually, I can imagine and can realize the appearance of God in front of me, or I can imagine his figure, but no one can see God. It's my limit.

"Space people? I don't know"

ISONO

OK. Do you believe or do you accept space people?

SPIRIT 1

Space people? Space people. Space people. I don't know.

ISONO

You don't know?

SPIRIT 1

I don't know.

ISONO

You said, "Believe in science."

SPIRIT 1

Yeah.

ISONO

So, according to the teachings of Happy Science, there are so many space people...

SPIRIT 1

Really?

ISONO

...outside the Earth, and they have advanced technology or civilization. They have advanced knowledge of science.

SPIRIT 1

But they have no emission of, they will not emit any CO_2, I guess so. If they are alive, they don't use CO_2, I think so. Their working force is quite different from ours, if aliens are real, but I cannot imagine.

ISONO

They are real. They have advanced technology, and some good or friendly space people will teach the earthlings how to balance their progress with maintaining the environment. Why don't you study or why don't you learn those knowledge or technology?

SPIRIT 1

Haha, I'm just a 16-year-old or so. I've never learned about aliens. Just I can see through movies, yeah. We can image aliens, but I've never studied. Modern science never says anything about aliens. So, it's possible, but we have no evidence.

My God is older than Israel's god, It's an ancient god of Scandinavia

YOSHII

You said you believe in Yahweh.

SPIRIT 1

Maybe.

YOSHII

"Maybe," OK.

SPIRIT 1

Maybe Yahweh or Jehovah-like existence.

YOSHII

One aspect of Yahweh is to be envious.

SPIRIT 1

Envious!?

YOSHII

Envious of human beings' progress. Do you feel envious of people prospering?

SPIRIT 1

Most powerful figure of my God is destroying bad people; perishing bad people and saving good people only.

ISONO

How can you tell good from bad? Who are the good people?

SPIRIT 1

People who obey God are good and people who deny God are bad.

ISONO

Are you saying that those who believe in Yahweh are good people, and those who don't believe in Yahweh are bad people?

SPIRIT 1
Yeah.

ISONO
Correct?

SPIRIT 1

Correct.

YOSHII

And those people are living in harmony with nature?

SPIRIT 1

But my God is maybe older, I mean an ancient existence. It's not Israel's god. It's older than that, ancient. Ancient god, maybe more ancient god. It's around the sky of the Scandinavian area. It's ancient.

YOSHII

Another question. I think you stick too much to using the word "science."

SPIRIT 1

Science.

YOSHII

I think in science, there are various theories, but in your case, there is one conclusion. Why do you use the word "science"?

SPIRIT 1

I can't accept Happy Science. I don't know such kind of "science." I just learn science through scientists' teachings only. And these 30 years, the conclusion is the same. Have you watched the film of Vice President Gore of the United States?* He already was a prophet of the modern society, but he lost in the presidential election, and the world is declining now.

---

* The spirit is talking about the movie, *An Inconvenient Truth* (Paramount Classics, 2006).

5

Asking about Japan and China

Xi Jinping is "a devil"

FUJII

At first, you told us that you don't like Prime Minister Abe.

SPIRIT 1

Prime Minister Abe is a devil. Devil. Maybe devil.

FUJII

Yes, yes. OK. How about Xi Jinping of China?

SPIRIT 1

Xi Jinping is also a devil.

FUJII

Devil. Why?

SPIRIT 1

Yeah. Devil, devil, devil. Devil versus devil.

FUJII

You don't like political leaders?

SPIRIT 1

Political leaders... hmm.

FUJII

You don't like them?

SPIRIT 1

If he or she is an eco-oriented person, I can accept him or her.

FUJII

What kind of politician do you like?

SPIRIT 1

Hmm.

FUJII

Obama?

SPIRIT 1

Angela Merkel-like person can understand me.

YOSHII

What do you think of President Obama? He promoted Green New Deal*.

SPIRIT 1

He is also a hypocrite. I mean, just speaking good things and doing bad things. He has two aspects.

YOSHII

So, Merkel was doing what she said, you mean?

SPIRIT 1

She will understand what I say.

---

* A policy that aims to create economic growth by investing into anti-global warming and other public purposes. It comes from Franklin Roosevelt's "New Deal" and the word "green."

He is not sure if he is the real Noah or not

ISONO

Do you remember having an interview with us before? [*A question to check whether Spirit 1 is Noah*]

SPIRIT 1

What?

ISONO

If you are the real Noah, this is the second time.*

SPIRIT 1

Really?

ISONO

Are you?

SPIRIT 1

It's a different Noah.

---

* Happy Science recorded a spiritual message from Noah, a prophet in the Old Testament, on July 10, 2014. See Ryuho Okawa, *Noah no Hakobune Densetsu wa Hontou ka* (lit. "Is the Legend of Noah's Ark True?") (Tokyo: IRH Press, 2014), available in Japanese.

ISONO

Different Noah? No!

SPIRIT 1

Yeah. Noah is a popular name, so there are a lot of Noahs.

ISONO

How can you prove you are the real Noah?

SPIRIT 1

I don't know, but I'm just the most fearful person about the global flooding, and I, myself, want to use a boat or a ship. It means I am the Noah of modern times.

ISONO

Or perhaps, you are a different Noah, aren't you?

SPIRIT 1

Oh, really? Hmm.

ISONO

Because the first time, Master Okawa summoned the spirit of Noah, and then he spoke. But this time, Master called some being who has the most influence on Greta Thunberg, and then you appeared.

SPIRIT 1

Uh huh. Yeah. But in the near future, I will be a Nobel Peace Prize laureate,* so I will have more influence all over the world than your Master Okawa. So, I'm very short distanced from God. I am.

---

* Greta Thunberg was allegedly a Nobel Peace Prize nominee for 2019, but she did not win it.

"Japanese are bad people"

FUJII

You mean, you are fighting against Master Ryuho Okawa?

SPIRIT 1

No, more than that. I'm just saying he is a bad, old guy also.

FUJII

Why do you think he is a bad guy?

SPIRIT 1

Because he is a Japanese. Japanese are bad people.

YOSHII

Why don't you like Japanese?

SPIRIT 1

Japan did nothing for the world.

ISONO

No, no, no.

SPIRIT 1

Only bad things, evil things for the world. Killing people and made occur the Second World War.

ISONO

But you, Swedish people, also fought a war against the Nazis or Russia. You fought and killed many people.

SPIRIT 1

Yeah. Just defense. Yeah, defense. Just defense.

ISONO

No, no, no. Japan also fought for defense.

SPIRIT 1

Really?

ISONO

We fought...

SPIRIT 1

Yeah, also, you were already aggressive. You were intrusion only. Expansion only. You are the predecessors of Xi Jinping.

YOSHII

Do you have a vivid memory of World War II? Or...

SPIRIT 1

Vivid memory! World War II? Oh, oh, oh, I'm more than 4,000 years old, so hmm...

YOSHII

I think you seem to hate even eco-oriented Japanese. You hate such Japanese.

SPIRIT 1

Is there any eco-oriented Japanese?

YOSHII

Yeah, I think there are various eco-oriented Japanese.

SPIRIT 1

Oh, really?

YOSHII

Do you like them?

SPIRIT 1

Are they real Japanese?

ISONO

Yes.

SPIRIT 1

Oh, really?

ISONO

For example, Ms. Yuriko Koike.

SPIRIT 1

Yuriko Koike?

ISONO

Governor of Tokyo. She is very much an environmentalist.

SPIRIT 1

If she were eco-oriented, she would destroy Tokyo. She would never hold the Tokyo Olympics.

ISONO

Umm, but she is seeking for the way to balance progress with protecting the environment.

SPIRIT 1

It's just advertisement, I think.

ISONO

But Japanese companies are now searching or studying a new way to eco-oriented technology. So, Japan is one of the most eco-friendly, advanced countries.

SPIRIT 1

No, I can't believe what you say.

ISONO

So, you should respect Japan.

SPIRIT 1

I cannot, I cannot. You are bad people, and I cannot believe that. You never think about Sweden or Norway or such kind of Scandinavian people.

ISONO

But you also don't think about the happiness of other nations' people.

SPIRIT 1

No... yeah, yeah, about the bad deeds of advanced countries, I think a lot, yeah.

His recognition of Odin

YOSHII

Where does your feeling of hatred toward Japanese come from?

SPIRIT 1

Hmm? My hatred?

YOSHII

Yeah, why?

SPIRIT 1

Hmm... Why, why, why, why, why... why, why. We are always confronted with Russia. Hmm... Japan, hmm... Russia was a bad country, has been a bad country for more than 2,000 years, yeah. In the ancient age, there was utopia in the north part of Europe, but it was destroyed by gigantic people from Russia, I've heard so.

YOSHII

Do you have a memory of having lived in north Europe at that time?

SPIRIT 1

North Europe, yeah. That kind of gigantic people came, climbed over the mountains of Ural, and intruded Europe. They attacked the north part of Europe, the Scandinavian area and Great Britain area, and almost Germany, around that.

ISONO

Have you ever heard of a god named Odin*?

---

* Odin is the chief god of Norse mythology. Based on spiritual research by Happy Science, he was a real king of Asgard who lived about 8,000 to 9,000 years ago. He established a civilization that was mainly in Northern Europe. Odin is one of the branch spirits of El Cantare, God of the Earth. See Ryuho Okawa, *Mighty Thor to Odin no Hokuo Shinwa wo Reisa suru* (lit. "Spiritually Investigating the Norse Mythology of Mighty Thor and Odin") (Tokyo: IRH Press, 2017), available in Japanese.

SPIRIT 1

Ah... Odin. Hmm, Odin. Odin, Odin. Hmm, Odin was once a king of the iceberg island or so, I've heard. But it was before the worldwide flooding. I think so.

ISONO

Do you like Odin?

SPIRIT 1

I don't know Odin, but hmm... Odin, if there were Odin, he might be the origin of the Vikings.

YOSHII

Even Vikings...

SPIRIT 1

Vikings.

YOSHII

It means Odin created some civilization. That's why you think so?

SPIRIT 1

No, no. Ship to steal something from other countries or people. Vikings' king, king of the Vikings.

Technology will destroy the Earth

YOSHII

Your ideal situation is where you live peacefully with nature.

SPIRIT 1

Yeah, in the log cabin. In a log cabin, yeah.

YOSHII

In a quiet area.

SPIRIT 1

Yeah.

YOSHII

With very few people.

SPIRIT 1

And don't use any money. And a nature-friendly culture.

YOSHII

Yeah, I would like to respect your opinion, your thinking. So, is there any way... There are various people and various concepts, so I think there is a way for us to live together.

SPIRIT 1

No, no. You know, they are pest-like people. They have pests within them.

YOSHII

So, you mean, making use of technology makes people...

SPIRIT 1

It's just a direction toward destroying this Earth.

ISONO

Are you the only existence who has influence on Greta Thunberg? Or, is there any other existence?

SPIRIT 1

Any other existence on Greta Thunberg... Hmm. Additional one, there is.

ISONO

Who is it?

SPIRIT 1

Call, please call.

6

Another Spirit behind Miss Greta Thunberg's Actions

The spirit who calls himself The "only God" appears

RYUHO OKAWA

OK. Is there anyone? The spirit who speaks he is Noah, Saint Noah, the old prophet Noah, said so. Is there anyone who has influence on Greta Thunberg from Sweden? Is there anyone who has influence on her? Is there anyone who has influence on her?

[*24 seconds of silence.*]

SPIRIT 2
Hmm.

ISONO
Hello.

SPIRIT 2

Ah?

ISONO

Can you hear me?

SPIRIT 2

Yeah.

ISONO

Can you speak?

SPIRIT 2

Yeah. Ah?

FUJII

Are you feeling happy? Or not? Are you feeling happy or not?

SPIRIT 2

I can't understand. Happy, what is happy? Hmm?

ISONO

Can you tell us your name?

SPIRIT 2

Name?

ISONO

Name. Your name.

SPIRIT 2

Hmm? Hmm... Hmm? [*Questions himself for 56 seconds.*] Hmm.

YOSHII

Are you thinking of something?

SPIRIT 2

Hmm?

YOSHII

Are you thinking?

SPIRIT 2

Hmm. I am the God.

ISONO

You are the God?

SPIRIT 2

Uh huh.

ISONO

"The" God?

SPIRIT 2

Uh, "the" God. Only God. Just sleeping.

The leader of the Russian Revolution
Declares the resurrection of Russia

ISONO

Then, you must have a name.

SPIRIT 2

Umm.

ISONO

Could you please tell us your name?

SPIRIT 2

Lenin [see Figure 2].

Figure 2.
Vladimir Lenin (1870 - 1924)
A Russian revolutionary and politician who started his revolutionary activities when he was still in school. After the Russian Revolution in 1917, he established the Union of Soviet Socialist Republics (Soviet Union, USSR) and became its first leader.

ISONO

Sorry?

FUJII

Lenin?

LENIN

Lenin.

ISONO

Lenin from Russia.

LENIN

Russia. King. Yeah.

ISONO

And you have influence on Greta Thunberg.

LENIN

Yeah, to destroy other countries.

ISONO

Why did you choose her?

LENIN

She is one possibility. People will hear a 16-year-old girl's voice. It's a genuine word, no calculation. So, believe in her. She will be a great world teacher. She wants to destroy America, China, Japan, Germany, France. [*Laughs.*]

ISONO

She also hates Russia.

LENIN

No, no, no. No, no, it's not, it's not. No. Russia is making resurrection again.

FUJII

I think you were a leader of the Russian Revolution.

LENIN

Yeah.

FUJII

What was the meaning of...

LENIN

God of Russia.

FUJII

What was the purpose of your revolution?

LENIN

Yeah. Russia should be the center of the world.

FUJII

But you killed many people.

LENIN

No, no, no. We were killed by Hitler.

FUJII

Are you more than Hitler?

LENIN

I didn't kill so many people. I killed just millions of people, so it's quite few. Yeah, it's very few people.

ISONO

You said you are the God of Russia. And...

LENIN

And Scandinavian countries are under the control of Russia.

ISONO

Uh huh. Do you give inspiration to President Putin?

LENIN

President Putin? Umm... I don't have a good connection with him. He denies us. Yeah, I mean, Lenin and Stalin.

7

Why the Spirit Wants to
Spread the Global Warming Theory

Why he wants to stop the CO$_2$ emission
Of advanced countries

YOSHII

You destroyed several civilizations. What do you want to realize?

LENIN

My main point is, it's time for us, the northern part of the Earth that includes snow and ice. It's our age. Yeah. We must be the center. So, I want to stop the modern development of other countries.

ISONO

So, you want to stop the progress of other countries by using the global warming problem, correct?

LENIN

Yeah. Yeah, yeah. If they use CO_2 more and more, it will make the global warming; it will make the Earth hotter and hotter, and it will prevent the "iceberg age"* from coming. If the iceberg age comes, they will be under... their civilization will be under the ice, and we will be a Greenland-like country. Yeah. "Green-full" country.

YOSHII

I think just stopping the progress of other countries, other civilizations, will not be enough to make the north part of Europe including Russia prosper. What do you think about that?

LENIN

Yeah. I think that the next age, next civilization will come in the near future, and at that time, Russia and Scandinavian people will be the center of the

---

* The spirit used the term "iceberg age." It is left as it was spoken.

world. The other people, some will be of course under the worldwide flooding, and others will be under the iceberg. Yeah. Climate change is just a plan by us.

YOSHII

So, you have spiritual influence on the real climate change?

LENIN

Yeah. If I can succeed in stopping using the oil or gas or other CO_2 emissions, the economic growth of other countries will stop, and Russia will be the center of the next century. Hmm.

YOSHII

I think if Russia were the center of the world, there would need to be a tool to rule other countries. To rule other countries, I think you need some technologies. So, I mean...

LENIN

No, no, no, they would just perish. They would be perished, and we would survive and we can control our country and our followers.

YOSHII

So, the political system with you as the emperor is totalitarianism?

LENIN

Not totalitarian. One country system.

YOSHII

So, one country system is, the system itself is very similar to China's political system.

LENIN

No, no. China is finished with its destiny already. Japan also, and the United States of America and India, also. They will be perished because of the greater population problem, and they should die.

We are the next emergent, the next people who have sovereignty over this world.

FUJII

So, you mean the global warming theory is just a tool to stop...

LENIN

Yeah. Tool.

FUJII

...the other countries' progress?

LENIN

Another tool. Another tool to kill advanced countries, stop them, and make them decline. Yeah.

FUJII

You don't believe in global warming theory, actually?

LENIN

Ahaha. Global warming theory...

FUJII

You don't believe it? It's just a tool?

LENIN

...is not correct. Yeah. It was 10,000 years ago, which started in the end of the eternal ice age, and there became the warm climate these 10,000 years. Next will come the iceberg age again, and at that time, we can live in a warm country, but some other countries will be underwater and some will be under the iceberg. The pole will shift in the near future, I think. I'm aiming at not changing the climate, but I'm aiming at changing the Earth's condition. I, once, was the enemy of Odin, so I will be the next king of this Earth.

Greta will be "a new Christ"

YOSHII

OK. So, your dream is to make more people obey
you.

LENIN

Uh huh.

YOSHII

Is that your top priority?

LENIN

Obey?

YOSHII

Obey, or make people follow you.

LENIN

Ah. No, no, no. Just Greta Thunberg says something,
and people will somewhat obey her. She will be a

new Christ in the near future, in the area of climate change and global warming. New religious leader, she will be, and she will perish Happy Science, of course. This is the end of you.

YOSHII

So now, you are the most powerful teacher to her.

LENIN

Yeah, I'm God. Just God. I am using our Noah, and through Noah, to her.

ISONO

Was it the real Noah who spoke before you came?

LENIN

There are a lot of Noahs.

ISONO

A lot of Noahs.

LENIN

Yeah.

FUJII

Just a messenger for you?

LENIN

[*Sighs.*]

FUJII

Is this the casting for this world?

LENIN

He was my disciple. One of my disciples of the old age (in my past life). He admired me.

"Climate change revolution" for the people of The north part of the Earth

LENIN

Don't you think that this is possible or it is recommendable that the Scandinavian area and the north part of Russia become the center of the Earth, that the other countries are declining and finish their histories, and that the history of the Earth will be changed or rewritten by other people?

ISONO

We know that the center of the world has been changing for a very long time.

LENIN

Uh huh.

ISONO

But today, this time, the United States and Japan are the center of the world now.

LENIN

No, no, no.

ISONO

We think so.

LENIN

Finished already.

ISONO

No, no.

LENIN

And China will be finished.

ISONO

By following Master Okawa's teachings, the U.S. and Japan will create the golden age.

LENIN

No, no, no, no. It's a dream, just a dream. She has a dream, also. Her dream, only 16-year-old young girl's. Her dream.

YOSHII

There are various young activists around the world now. How do you define your revolution?

LENIN

Ah! The first step is to destroy the advanced countries, and next is to make new powers occur from the north part of the Earth, yeah. They are suffering a lot by dint of snow or ice or cold weather, so it's time.

YOSHII

So, it's one kind of climate change revolution.

LENIN

Yeah, climate change revolution. So, the people who are living in the cold area will be the next champion of the world. This is the main point. So, you are dying.

ISONO

OK. Now, we could understand the basic concept of your thinking. I think this is enough for today.

LENIN

Oh, really?

ISONO

Yes. Maybe...

LENIN

Then, you really got the name of the real God, yeah. Yeah, it's great for you, great discovery. It's a resurrection of Lenin.

ISONO

Uh huh.

LENIN

Yeah.

ISONO

Thank you very much. Thank you for today.

LENIN

Greta is a fighting girl like the... yeah, the French...

ISONO

Jeanne d'Arc (Joan of Arc)?

LENIN

...Jeanne d'Arc-like fighting lady for climate change. She believes in the theory, so it's lucky for me to use her, yeah.

ISONO

OK. Thank you very much.

LENIN

Is it enough?

ISONO

Yes.

LENIN

OK. Ha, your real God's name is Lenin, yeah.

ISONO

OK, thank you very much.

8

After the Spiritual Interviews

RYUHO OKAWA

OK, thank you, bye-bye [*claps four times*].

Ah. Hmm. The truth is a little different. I think global warming started about 10,000 years ago. At that time, the north part of the Earth was covered with snow and ice, and after the global warming started, there occurred the green area in the north part... for example, the U.K. and the Scandinavian area and some part of the Russian area. At that time, there appeared Odin's ideal country. Odin's name is very famous.

After that, there came another civilization. It was in the south part of Europe, around the Mediterranean Sea. It was made by Hermes* and

---

* One of the Olympian gods of Greek Mythology. He was a real hero of Greece 4,300 years ago. He is a branch spirit of El Cantare, God of the Earth, who taught teachings of love and progress and brought prosperity all over Greece.

Zeus*, around Egypt or Greece and Italy. Next were Israel and the other parts of Europe, and of course, another pole was the Asian part like China and Japan.

So, yeah, this is maybe indeed the collision of civilizations. Greta Thunberg is indeed the messenger of expansionism from the north part of the Earth. One is Russia, and the Scandinavian countries, also. So, I can understand their desire.

But they should know that, at that time, their God was Odin, not Yahweh. They had already mistaken their God's name, I think.

So, my conclusion is that Greta has very keen attention to climate justice and cutting the emission of CO_2, but she is one tool of a demonish god. Now another collision of civilizations is occurring. They are expecting that.

But Vladimir Putin has a little different opinion. We have much concern about Russia, and we should

---

* The main Olympian god of Greek Mythology. He was a real person who ruled Greece 3,600 years ago. He is one of the grand spirits of the ninth dimension, the highest world for human souls.

be friends with Russia and make Russia come into the Western society. I said G7 should add one country, Russia, into G8 again, I recommended so, and President Trump and Prime Minister Abe also recommended so.

So, this is really a problem of the future of Russia, yeah. In the Russian area, there is some kind of hope to be the champion of the world. There are Lenin and Stalin, these two devils have influence on Russia and other countries, so we must prepare for them.

Ah, I got one conclusion. So, this is the reason why. Thank you very much.

Afterword

We already know that there is a China-related group behind the left wing environmental activist Ms. Greta. Of course, this is not something that a 16-year-old girl can do. The purpose is to prevent President Trump from becoming re-elected. China, which is causing the most problems with CO_2 emission, is urging this.

Also, in this book, we found that the spirit of Lenin, the leader of the Russian Revolution, is behind the scene.

I mean that Greta's activity only seems righteous, but is actually a "Communism Revival Movement" disguised as environmental liberalism. Ask yourself, who will benefit by pressuring the liberalist and capitalist countries to eliminating CO_2 emissions completely by 2050? You'll realize who this is if you think about that. You mustn't be deceived. The issue is not about "Climate Justice" but about "World Justice."

Ryuho Okawa
Master & CEO of Happy Science Group
Oct. 25, 2019

ABOUT THE AUTHOR

Founder and CEO of Happy Science Group.

Ryuho Okawa was born on July 7th 1956, in Tokushima, Japan. After graduating from the University of Tokyo with a law degree, he joined a Tokyo-based trading house. While working at its New York headquarters, he studied international finance at the Graduate Center of the City University of New York. In 1981, he attained Great Enlightenment and became aware that he is El Cantare with a mission to bring salvation to all humankind.

In 1986, he established Happy Science. It now has members in over 165 countries across the world, with more than 700 branches and temples as well as 10,000 missionary houses around the world.

He has given over 3,400 lectures (of which more than 150 are in English) and published over 3,000 books (of which more than 600 are Spiritual Interview Series), and many are translated into 40 languages. Along with *The Laws of the Sun* and *The Laws Of Messiah*, many of the books have become best sellers or million sellers. To date, Happy Science has produced 25 movies. The original story and original concept were given by the Executive Producer Ryuho Okawa. He has also composed music and written lyrics of over 450 pieces.

Moreover, he is the Founder of Happy Science University and Happy Science Academy (Junior and Senior High School), Founder and President of the Happiness Realization Party, Founder and Honorary Headmaster of Happy Science Institute of Government and Management, Founder of IRH Press Co., Ltd., and the Chairperson of NEW STAR PRODUCTION Co., Ltd. and ARI Production Co., Ltd.

WHAT IS EL CANTARE?

El Cantare means "the Light of the Earth," and is the Supreme God of the Earth who has been guiding humankind since the beginning of Genesis. He is whom Jesus called Father and Muhammad called Allah, and is *Ame-no-Mioya-Gami*, Japanese Father God. Different parts of El Cantare's core consciousness have descended to Earth in the past, once as Alpha and another as Elohim. His branch spirits, such as Shakyamuni Buddha and Hermes, have descended to Earth many times and helped to flourish many civilizations. To unite various religions and to integrate various fields of study in order to build a new civilization on Earth, a part of the core consciousness has descended to Earth as Master Ryuho Okawa.

Alpha is a part of the core consciousness of El Cantare who descended to Earth around 330 million years ago. Alpha preached Earth's Truths to harmonize and unify Earth-born humans and space people who came from other planets.

Elohim is a part of El Cantare's core consciousness who descended to Earth around 150 million years ago. He gave wisdom, mainly on the differences of light and darkness, good and evil.

Ame-no-Mioya-Gami (Japanese Father God) is the Creator God and the Father God who appears in the ancient literature, *Hotsuma Tsutae*. It is believed that He descended on the foothills of Mt. Fuji about 30,000 years ago and built the Fuji dynasty, which is the root of the Japanese civilization. With justice as the central pillar, Ame-no-Mioya-Gami's teachings spread to ancient civilizations of other countries in the world.

Shakyamuni Buddha was born as a prince into the Shakya Clan in India around 2,600 years ago. When he was 29 years old, he renounced the world and sought enlightenment. He later attained Great Enlightenment and founded Buddhism.

Hermes is one of the 12 Olympian gods in Greek mythology, but the spiritual Truth is that he taught the teachings of love and progress around 4,300 years ago that became the origin of the current Western civilization. He is a hero that truly existed.

Ophealis was born in Greece around 6,500 years ago and was the leader who took an expedition to as far as Egypt. He is the God of miracles, prosperity, and arts, and is known as Osiris in the Egyptian mythology.

Rient Arl Croud was born as a king of the ancient Incan Empire around 7,000 years ago and taught about the mysteries of the mind. In the heavenly world, he is responsible for the interactions that take place between various planets.

Thoth was an almighty leader who built the golden age of the Atlantic civilization around 12,000 years ago. In the Egyptian mythology, he is known as god Thoth.

Ra Mu was a leader who built the golden age of the civilization of Mu around 17,000 years ago. As a religious leader and a politician, he ruled by uniting religion and politics.

WHAT IS A SPIRITUAL MESSAGE?

We are all spiritual beings living on this earth. The following is the mechanism behind Master Ryuho Okawa's spiritual messages.

1 You are a spirit

People are born into this world to gain wisdom through various experiences and return to the other world when their lives end. We are all spirits and repeat this cycle in order to refine our souls.

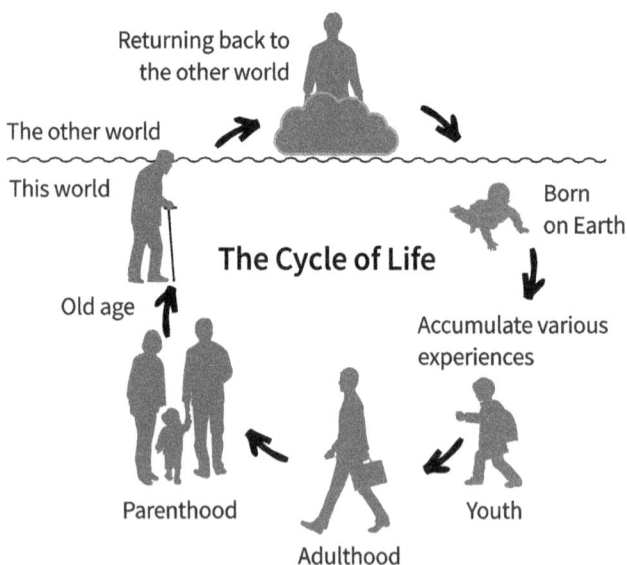

Returning back to the other world

The other world

This world

Born on Earth

The Cycle of Life

Old age

Accumulate various experiences

Parenthood

Adulthood

Youth

2 You have a guardian spirit

Guardian spirits are those who protect the people who are living on this earth. Each of us has a guardian spirit that watches over us and guides us from the other world. They were us in our past life, and are identical in how we think.

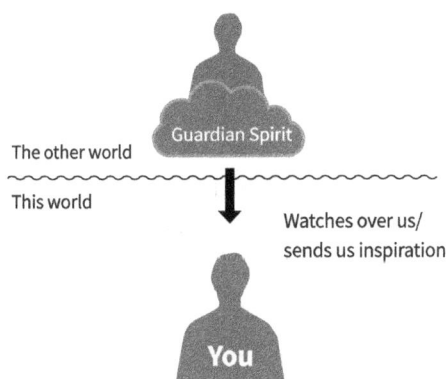

The other world

This world

Guardian Spirit

Watches over us/
sends us inspiration

You

3 How spiritual messages work

Master Ryuho Okawa, through his enlightenment, is capable of summoning any spirit from anywhere in the world, including the spirit world.

Master Okawa's way of receiving spiritual messages is fundamentally different from that of other psychic mediums who undergo trances and are thereby completely taken over by the spirits they are channeling.

Master Okawa's attainment of a high level of enlightenment enables him to retain full control of his consciousness and body throughout the duration of the spiritual message. To allow the spirits to express their own thoughts and personalities freely, however, Master Okawa usually softens the dominancy of his consciousness. This way, he is able to keep his own philosophies out of the way and ensure that the spiritual messages are pure expressions of the spirits he is channeling.

Since guardian spirits think at the same subconscious level as the person living on earth, Master Okawa can summon the spirit and find out what the person on earth is actually thinking. If the person has already returned to the other world, the spirit can give messages to the people living on earth through Master Okawa.

Since 2009, many spiritual messages have been openly recorded by Master Okawa and published. Spiritual messages from the guardian spirits of people living today such as Donald Trump, former Japanese Prime Minister Shinzo Abe and Chinese President Xi Jinping, as well as spiritual messages sent from the spirit world by Jesus Christ, Muhammad, Thomas Edison, Mother Teresa, Steve Jobs and Nelson Mandela are just a tiny pack of spiritual messages that were published so far.

Domestically, in Japan, these spiritual messages are being read by a wide range of politicians and mass media, and the high-level contents of these books are delivering an impact even more on politics, news and public opinion. In recent years, there have been spiritual messages recorded in English, and

English translations are being done on the spiritual messages given in Japanese. These have been published overseas, one after another, and have started to shake the world.

1 The guardian spirit / spirit in the other world...

2 Goes inside Master Okawa in this world

3 Master Okawa speaks the words of the guardian spirit / spirit

For more about spiritual messages and a complete list of books in the Spiritual Interview Series, visit okawabooks.com

ABOUT HAPPY SCIENCE

Happy Science is a global movement that empowers individuals to find purpose and spiritual happiness and to share that happiness with their families, societies, and the world. With more than 12 million members around the world, Happy Science aims to increase awareness of spiritual truths and expand our capacity for love, compassion, and joy so that together we can create the kind of world we all wish to live in.

Activities at Happy Science are based on the Principle of Happiness (Love, Wisdom, Self-Reflection, and Progress). This principle embraces worldwide philosophies and beliefs, transcending boundaries of culture and religions.

Love teaches us to give ourselves freely without expecting anything in return; it encompasses giving, nurturing, and forgiving.

Wisdom leads us to the insights of spiritual truths, and opens us to the true meaning of life and the will of God (the universe, the highest power, Buddha).

Self-Reflection brings a mindful, nonjudgmental lens to our thoughts and actions to help us find our truest selves—the essence of our souls—and deepen our connection to the highest power. It helps us attain a clean and peaceful mind and leads us to the right life path.

Progress emphasizes the positive, dynamic aspects of our spiritual growth—actions we can take to manifest and spread happiness around the world. It's a path that not only expands our soul growth, but also furthers the collective potential of the world we live in.

PROGRAMS AND EVENTS

The doors of Happy Science are open to all. We offer a variety of programs and events, including self-exploration and self-growth programs, spiritual seminars, meditation and contemplation sessions, study groups, and book events.

Our programs are designed to:
* Deepen your understanding of your purpose and meaning in life
* Improve your relationships and increase your capacity to love unconditionally
* Attain peace of mind, decrease anxiety and stress, and feel positive
* Gain deeper insights and a broader perspective on the world
* Learn how to overcome life's challenges
  ... and much more.

For more information, visit <u>happy-science.org</u>.

OUR ACTIVITIES

Happy Science does other various activities to provide support for those in need.

◆ **You Are An Angel! General Incorporated Association**

Happy Science has a volunteer network in Japan that encourages and supports children with disabilities as well as their parents and guardians.

◆ **Never Mind School for Truancy**

At 'Never Mind,' we support students who find it very challenging to attend schools in Japan. We also nurture their self-help spirit and power to rebound against obstacles in life based on Master Okawa's teachings and faith.

◆ **"Prevention Against Suicide" Campaign since 2003**

A nationwide campaign to reduce suicides; over 20,000 people commit suicide every year in Japan. "The Suicide Prevention Website-Words of Truth for You-" presents spiritual prescriptions for worries such as depression, lost love, extramarital affairs, bullying and work-related problems, thereby saving many lives.

◆ **Support for Anti-bullying Campaigns**

Happy Science provides support for a group of parents and guardians, Network to Protect Children from Bullying, a general incorporated foundation launched in Japan to end bullying, including those that can even be called a criminal offense. So far, the network received more than 5,000 cases and resolved 90% of them.

- **The Golden Age Scholarship**

This scholarship is granted to students who can contribute greatly and bring a hopeful future to the world.

- **Success No.1**
  Buddha's Truth Afterschool Academy

Happy Science has over 180 classrooms throughout Japan and in several cities around the world that focus on afterschool education for children. The education focuses on faith and morals in addition to supporting children's school studies.

- **Angel Plan V**

For children under the age of kindergarten, Happy Science holds classes for nurturing healthy, positive, and creative boys and girls.

- **Future Stars Training Department**

The Future Stars Training Department was founded within the Happy Science Media Division with the goal of nurturing talented individuals to become successful in the performing arts and entertainment industry.

- **NEW STAR PRODUCTION Co., Ltd.**
  ARI Production Co., Ltd.

We have companies to nurture actors and actresses, artists, and vocalists. They are also involved in film production.

CONTACT INFORMATION

Happy Science is a worldwide organization with branches and temples around the globe. For a comprehensive list, visit the worldwide directory at *happy-science.org*. The following are some of the many Happy Science locations:

UNITED STATES AND CANADA

New York
79 Franklin St., New York, NY 10013, USA
Phone: 1-212-343-7972
Fax: 1-212-343-7973
Email: ny@happy-science.org
Website: happyscience-usa.org

New Jersey
66 Hudson St., #2R, Hoboken, NJ 07030, USA
Phone: 1-201-313-0127
Email: nj@happy-science.org
Website: happyscience-usa.org

Chicago
2300 Barrington Rd., Suite #400,
Hoffman Estates, IL 60169, USA
Phone: 1-630-937-3077
Email: chicago@happy-science.org
Website: happyscience-usa.org

Florida
5208 8th St., Zephyrhills, FL 33542, USA
Phone: 1-813-715-0000
Fax: 1-813-715-0010
Email: florida@happy-science.org
Website: happyscience-usa.org

Atlanta
1874 Piedmont Ave., NE Suite 360-C
Atlanta, GA 30324, USA
Phone: 1-404-892-7770
Email: atlanta@happy-science.org
Website: happyscience-usa.org

San Francisco
525 Clinton St.
Redwood City, CA 94062, USA
Phone & Fax: 1-650-363-2777
Email: sf@happy-science.org
Website: happyscience-usa.org

Los Angeles
1590 E. Del Mar Blvd., Pasadena, CA
91106, USA
Phone: 1-626-395-7775
Fax: 1-626-395-7776
Email: la@happy-science.org
Website: happyscience-usa.org

Orange County
16541 Gothard St. Suite 104
Huntington Beach, CA 92647
Phone: 1-714-659-1501
Email: oc@happy-science.org
Website: happyscience-usa.org

San Diego
7841 Balboa Ave. Suite #202
San Diego, CA 92111, USA
Phone: 1-626-395-7775
Fax: 1-626-395-7776
E-mail: sandiego@happy-science.org
Website: happyscience-usa.org

Hawaii
Phone: 1-808-591-9772
Fax: 1-808-591-9776
Email: hi@happy-science.org
Website: happyscience-usa.org

Kauai
3343 Kanakolu Street, Suite 5
Lihue, HI 96766, USA
Phone: 1-808-822-7007
Fax: 1-808-822-6007
Email: kauai-hi@happy-science.org
Website: happyscience-usa.org

Toronto
845 The Queensway
Etobicoke, ON M8Z 1N6, Canada
Phone: 1-416-901-3747
Email: toronto@happy-science.org
Website: happy-science.ca

Vancouver
#201-2607 East 49th Avenue,
Vancouver, BC, V5S 1J9, Canada
Phone: 1-604-437-7735
Fax: 1-604-437-7764
Email: vancouver@happy-science.org
Website: happy-science.ca

INTERNATIONAL

Tokyo
1-6-7 Togoshi, Shinagawa,
Tokyo, 142-0041, Japan
Phone: 81-3-6384-5770
Fax: 81-3-6384-5776
Email: tokyo@happy-science.org
Website: happy-science.org

Seoul
74, Sadang-ro 27-gil,
Dongjak-gu, Seoul, Korea
Phone: 82-2-3478-8777
Fax: 82-2-3478-9777
Email: korea@happy-science.org
Website: happyscience-korea.org

London
3 Margaret St.
London, W1W 8RE United Kingdom
Phone: 44-20-7323-9255
Fax: 44-20-7323-9344
Email: eu@happy-science.org
Website: www.happyscience-uk.org

Taipei
No. 89, Lane 155, Dunhua N. Road,
Songshan District, Taipei City 105, Taiwan
Phone: 886-2-2719-9377
Fax: 886-2-2719-5570
Email: taiwan@happy-science.org
Website: happyscience-tw.org

Sydney
516 Pacific Highway, Lane Cove North,
2066 NSW, Australia
Phone: 61-2-9411-2877
Fax: 61-2-9411-2822
Email: sydney@happy-science.org

Kuala Lumpur
No 22A, Block 2, Jalil Link Jalan Jalil
Jaya 2, Bukit Jalil 57000,
Kuala Lumpur, Malaysia
Phone: 60-3-8998-7877
Fax: 60-3-8998-7977
Email: malaysia@happy-science.org
Website: happyscience.org.my

Sao Paulo
Rua. Domingos de Morais 1154,
Vila Mariana, Sao Paulo SP
CEP 04010-100, Brazil
Phone: 55-11-5088-3800
Email: sp@happy-science.org
Website: happyscience.com.br

Kathmandu
Kathmandu Metropolitan City,
Ward No. 15, Ring Road, Kimdol,
Sitapaila Kathmandu, Nepal
Phone: 977-1-427-2931
Email: nepal@happy-science.org

Jundiai
Rua Congo, 447, Jd. Bonfiglioli
Jundiai-CEP, 13207-340, Brazil
Phone: 55-11-4587-5952
Email: jundiai@happy-science.org

Kampala
Plot 877 Rubaga Road, Kampala
P.O. Box 34130 Kampala, UGANDA
Phone: 256-79-4682-121
Email: uganda@happy-science.org

ABOUT HS PRESS

HS Press is an imprint of IRH Press Co., Ltd. IRH Press Co., Ltd., based in Tokyo, was founded in 1987 as a publishing division of Happy Science. IRH Press publishes religious and spiritual books, journals, magazines and also operates broadcast and film production enterprises. For more information, visit *okawabooks.com*.

Follow us on:

f Facebook: Okawa Books
▶ Youtube: Okawa Books
𝓟 Pinterest: Okawa Books

⊙ Instagram: OkawaBooks
🐦 Twitter: Okawa Books
g Goodreads: Ryuho Okawa

——— **NEWSLETTER** ———

To receive book related news, promotions and events, please subscribe to our newsletter below.

🔗 eepurl.com/bsMeJj

——— **AUDIO / VISUAL MEDIA** ———

YOUTUBE

PODCAST

Introduction of Ryuho Okawa's titles; topics ranging from self-help, current affairs, spirituality, religion, and the universe.

BOOKS BY RYUHO OKAWA

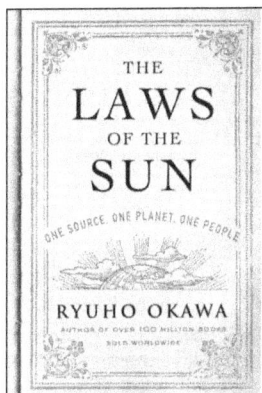

THE LAWS OF THE SUN
ONE SOURCE, ONE PLANET, ONE PEOPLE

Paperback • 288 pages • $15.95
ISBN: 978-1-942125-43-3

IMAGINE IF YOU COULD ASK GOD why He created this world and what spiritual laws He used to shape us—and everything around us. If we could understand His designs and intentions, we could discover what our goals in life should be and whether our actions move us closer to those goals or farther away.

At a young age, a spiritual calling prompted Ryuho Okawa to outline what he innately understood to be universal truths for all humankind. In *The Laws of the Sun*, Okawa outlines these laws of the universe and provides a road map for living one's life with greater purpose and meaning.

In this powerful book, Ryuho Okawa reveals the transcendent nature of consciousness and the secrets of our multidimensional universe and our place in it. By understanding the different stages of love and following the Buddhist Eightfold Path, he believes we can speed up our eternal process of development. *The Laws of the Sun* shows the way to realize true happiness—a happiness that continues from this world through the other.

For a complete list of books, visit **okawabooks.com**

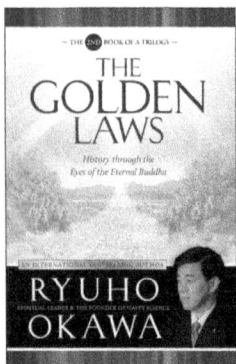

THE GOLDEN LAWS

HISTORY THROUGH THE EYES OF THE ETERNAL BUDDHA

Paperback • 201 pages • $14.95
ISBN: 978-1-941779-81-1

Throughout history, Great Guiding Spirits of Light have been present on Earth in both the East and the West at crucial points in human history to further our spiritual development. *The Golden Laws* reveals how Divine Plan has been unfolding on Earth, and outlines 5,000 years of the secret history of humankind. Once we understand the true course of history, through past, present and into the future, we cannot help but become aware of the significance of our spiritual mission in the present age.

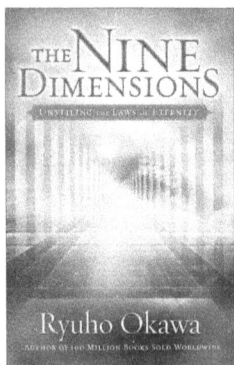

THE NINE DIMENSIONS

UNVEILING THE LAWS OF ETERNITY

Paperback • 168 pages • $15.95
ISBN: 978-0-982698-56-3

This book is a window into the mind of our loving God, who designed this world and the vast, wondrous world of our afterlife as a school with many levels through which our souls learn and grow. When the religions and cultures of the world discover the truth of their common spiritual origin, they will be inspired to accept their differences, come together under faith in God, and build an era of harmony and peaceful progress on Earth.

For a complete list of books, visit okawabooks.com

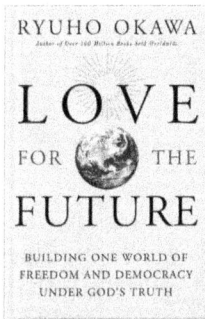

LOVE FOR THE FUTURE

BUILDING ONE WORLD OF FREEDOM AND DEMOCRACY UNDER GOD'S TRUTH

Paperback • 312 pages • $15.95
ISBN: 978-1-942125-60-0

This is a compilation of select international lectures given by Ryuho Okawa during his (ongoing) global missionary tours. It espouses that freedom and democracy are vital principles to foster peace and shared prosperity, if adopted universally.

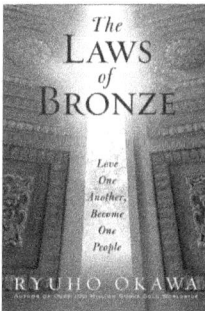

THE LAWS OF BRONZE

LOVE ONE ANOTHER, BECOME ONE PEOPLE

Paperback • 224 pages • $15.95
ISBN: 978-1-942125-50-1

This is the 25th volume of the Laws Series by Ryuho Okawa. This miraculous and inspiring book will show the keys to living a spiritual life of truth regardless of their age, gender, or race.

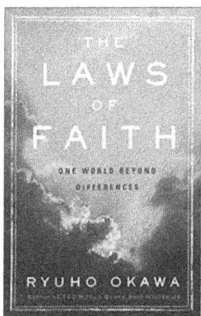

THE LAWS OF FAITH

ONE WORLD BEYOND DIFFERENCES

Paperback • 208 pages • $15.95
ISBN: 978-1-942125-34-1

Ryuho Okawa preaches at the core of a new universal religion from various angles while integrating logical and spiritual viewpoints in mind with current world situations. This book offers us the key to accept diversities beyond differences to create a world filled with peace and prosperity.

*For a complete list of books, visit **okawabooks.com***

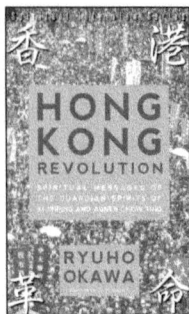

HONG KONG REVOLUTION

SPIRITUAL MESSAGES OF THE GUARDIAN SPIRITS OF XI JINPING AND AGNES CHOW TING

Paperback • 282 pages • $13.95
ISBN: 978-1-943869-55-8

The Hong Kong protests that are gathering the attention of the world. What is Xi Jinping plotting? How far is Agnes Chow, the 'Goddess of Democracy,' willing to go? Their guardian spirits sreveal issues of conflict in this exciting new book!

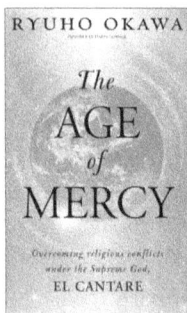

THE AGE OF MERCY

OVERCOMING RELIGIOUS CONFLICTS UNDER THE SUPREME GOD, EL CANTARE

Hardcover • 110 pages • $22.95
ISBN: 978-1-943869-51-0

Why are there conflicts in the world? How can people understand each other better? This book is a message from the Supreme God who has been guiding humankind from the beginning of creation.

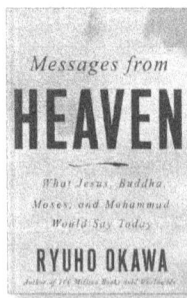

MESSAGES FROM HEAVEN

WHAT JESUS, BUDDHA, MOSES, AND MUHAMMAD WOULD SAY TODAY

Hardcover • 214 pages • $19.95
ISBN: 978-1-941779-19-4

If you could speak to Jesus, Buddha, Moses, or Muhammad, what would you ask? Ryuho Okawa uses his spiritual power to communicate with these four spirits and shares their messages to the people living today.

For a complete list of books, visit **okawabooks.com**

SPIRITUAL INTERVIEW SERIES

Spiritual Messages from Oscar Wilde
Love, Beauty, and LGBT

Margaret Thatcher's Miraculous Message
An Interview with the Iron Lady 19 Hours After Her Death

The Trump Secret
Seeing Through the Past, Present,
and Future of the New American President

7 Future Predictions
Spiritual Interview with the
Guardian Spirit of Henry Kissinger

Spiritual Interview with the
Guardian Spirit of Malala Yousafzai
A Wind of Hope for the Islamic World

A New Message from Barack Obama
Interviewing the Guardian Spirit of
the President of the United States

Steve Jobs Returns with His Secrets
Be Simple, Be Crazy

For the Future of Thailand and Japan
Interviewing the Guardian Spirit of Yingluck Shinawatra

Samurai President of the Philippines
Spiritual Interview with the
Guardian Spirit of Rodrigo Duterte

Spiritual Interview with Liu Xiaobo
The Fight for Freedom Continues

The Genius of Ichiro
The Secret Behind His Four Thousand Hits

Nelson Mandela's Last Message to the World
A Conversation with Madiba Six Hours After His Death

For a complete list of books, visit **okawabooks.com**

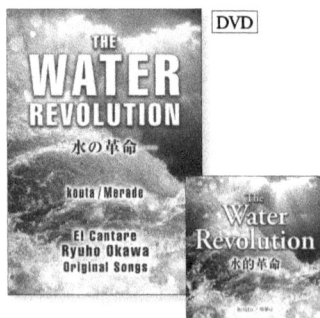

With Savior *English version*

This is the message of hope to the modern people who are living in the midst of the Coronavirus pandemic, natural disasters, economic depression, and other various crises.

Search on YouTube

with savior 🔍 for a short ad!

CD

The Thunder

a composition for repelling the Coronavirus

We have been granted this music from our Lord. It will repel away the novel Coronavirus originated in China. Experience this magnificent powerful music.

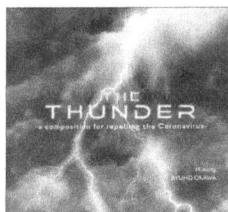

Search on YouTube

the thunder composition 🔍

for a short ad!

CD

The Exorcism

prayer music for repelling Lost Spirits

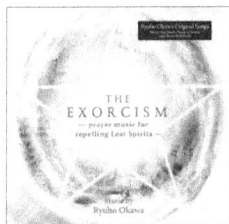

Feel the divine vibrations of this Japanese and Western exorcising symphony to banish all evil possessions you suffer from and to purify your space!

Search on YouTube

the exorcism repelling 🔍

for a short ad!

CD

Listen now today!

Download from
Spotify iTunes Amazon

DVD, CD available at amazon.com,
and Happy Science locations worldwide

133

www.ingramcontent.com/pod-product-compliance
Lightning Source LLC
Chambersburg PA
CBHW032059020426
42335CB00011B/418